Contents

Introduction

Going barefoot is the gentlest way of walking and can symbolise a way of living — being authentic, vulnerable, sensitive to our surroundings. It's enjoying the feeling of warm sand beneath our toes, or carefully making our way over sharp rocks in the darkness. It's a way of living that has the lightest impact, removing the barrier between us and nature.

Getting in touch with our Dreamtime, our origins, gives us a connection with the land — the rain, wind, trees, creatures, oceans and sky. This brings a deeply spiritual quality to our place on the earth. It makes our life a dance that moves with the ancient rhythms of what gave birth to the stars. Our own dreaming will have an integrity and a pattern that is harmonious with the source of *life* itself.

A personal harmony with the Creator gives strength to my own dreaming, as well as the conviction of my solemn responsibility as a human being: to take better care of the life that remains on earth. The Bible says a lot about our relationship with nature, but I believe this has been widely misunderstood. The concept of 'dominion' has been used by many as an excuse to do what they like with the land and its creatures, while piously waiting for heaven to enjoy a respectful relationship with nature. But this denies our responsibility to the rest of creation now. You can't walk barefoot blindly.

These poems and photographs are dances of both joy and pain. They are celebrations of what is still so beautiful and unique in this land. They are earnest questions for truth through the ugliness. They are a call to live in harmony with the ancient rhythms and the pure colours of the earth.

To be a barefoot dreamer is to dance with toes firmly on the earth, but hands reaching up towards the stars. It means to link past to future, hopes to possibilities, perceptions to feelings. It is ultimately a life lived in harmony with creation and with integrity towards all creatures.

COLOURS OF AUSTRALIA

Red dawn from the beginning of her time,
ochre-red earth and life-blood.
Orange roar of the bushfire,
orange fire in her sunsets.
Yellow gold glows the wattle
and the song of the summer cicada.
Dusk-green are the eucalypts
and deep-green her surrounding oceans.

Blue is the true-blue of her skies
and the souls of all her dreamers.
Indigo is the night,
the cover for her sorrow.
Violet lifts the mountains
and holds the long summer evenings.
White shines her beaches, her edges,
and pale are her adopted daughters and sons.
Black is the pain of her native-born,
and the long, dark midnight before the dawn.

DIDGERIDOO

*Vibrates the deep rhythm of the heart and
    soul of this land,
sings with the ancient voice of humanity
    to the infinite Creator,
breathes spirit of the pain and joy of being,
gives voice to the unvoiced. . .*

*Gives song to the stars over Capricorn,
gives rhythm to the rock,
gives sound to hot blue sky,
music to a misty morning.*

*Gives voice to the emu and the goanna,
to twisted mulga and the huge rivergum,
to the growth of spinifex out of red sand,
and to kangaroos leaping through high grass
    at dawn.*

*Echoes the spirit of wind over clifftop
    and desert,
of dripping, breathing rainforest,
of ephemeral campfire flames
    on a deserted beach,
of beating hearts aching for
    a rhythm of peace.*

WARRUMBUNGLE BLUE

Set in this earth-place by earth-time,
steep jagged volcanic energy frozen still,
huge standing stones penetrate the blue,
encircling eagles for company.

Sounds of timeless stillness
surround and retreat
with sudden rushing wind;

trickling creek, elusive bird whistles,
kangaroos rustling grass, a falling branch,
a whirr of wings, another rush of wind.

Under the blue
the stillness gives dreaming
to this place,
till it moves one
beyond this place,
beyond this time.

A PLACE

There's a place I like to go
to think a bit.
When life becomes confusing and
*   gets me down.*
Beneath an overhanging sandstone rock
where drops of water echo.
Soft cool mud oozes up between my bare toes,
reminding me of where I came from.
Cold drops of water splash on my head
*   now and then*
to remind me who I am.
Swirling colours in the rock infuse design
into my world again.
And I feel like an Aborigine,
related to the rock,
belonging to the earth.
Peace and balance seep into my world again.
And I walk away from that place
with dried mud on my feet
and simplicity in my soul.

MOUNTAIN COMMUNION

As I walk out into the fine soft mist
floating gently through the mountain air,
my upturned face, my child-like dance,
my every breath is a prayer.

And the soft cool rain is your gentle answer,
your loving fingers touch my cheek,
and the moment is such holy joy
that I cannot speak.

THE DREAM

How tempting it is
to want a piece of this country —
to 'own' some of its space,
make our dreams come true,
build our heart's desire,
be it haven or empire,
and call it 'our place'.

But the land never belongs to us.
It's only lent with awesome freedom
to create and replenish,
or waste and strip bare.
What legacy will we leave
alongside our footprints?
What will be left to share?

Though it endures title-deed holders,
the land is never ours to keep.
Long after the proud 'owners' have gone,
merely campers moving on,
will the land still be here
to sustain our children?
Or will its fragile beauty be gone?

BEAUTIFUL FEET

Perhaps if we all took our shoes off,
people would see how we really walk.
They'd see the beauty of who we are,
what hides beneath clothes and faces —
all the cracks, knobbles and callouses.

Perhaps if we all walked barefoot,
we'd belong more securely to the earth.
We'd get dirty feet, we'd step more lightly
and be more sensitive to the pain and joy of being.

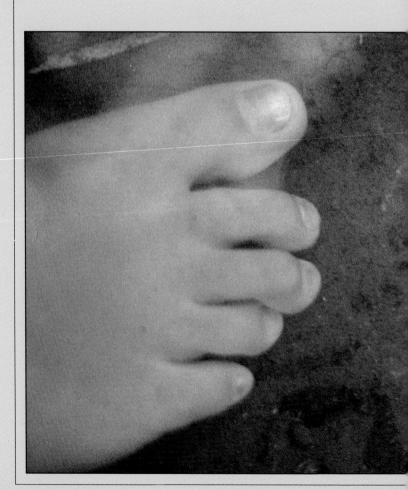

Perhaps if we danced barefoot,
our heels and toes would sing in harmony,
our laughter would not be hollow,
but pure and overflowing
with knowing the truth of beauty.

Perhaps if we walked in love
and not just talked it,
our footsteps would leave the earth a better place,
the world would see God and peace,
and we'd have beautiful feet.

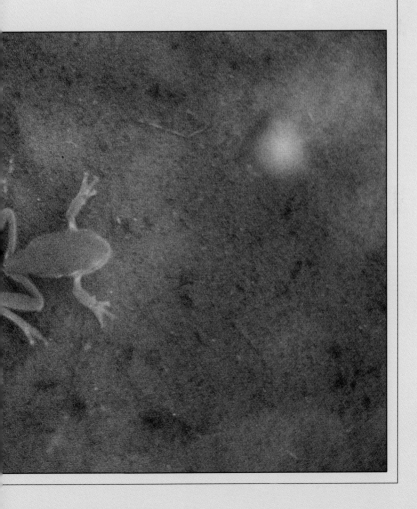

WIND

Whips through whispering casuarinas
flexing, bowing before its gusty force.
Bends, but does not always break.
Rushes through the tops of a stand of pines,
united in solid strength under its pressure,
holding complete stillness and warmth within.

Hear its sound, feel the surge
        of invisible power,
But strive not to know the mysteries
        of its source or destiny.
Only be reborn of Spirit.

Braces body, squares shoulder, renews skin,
untangles busy knots of confusion from
        my mind,
smooths deep forehead worry-grooves,
blows away anger, clutter, desire, distraction,
strips me bare of pretence,
leaves me clothed with trueness.
(It's only the evergreens who keep their leaves.)

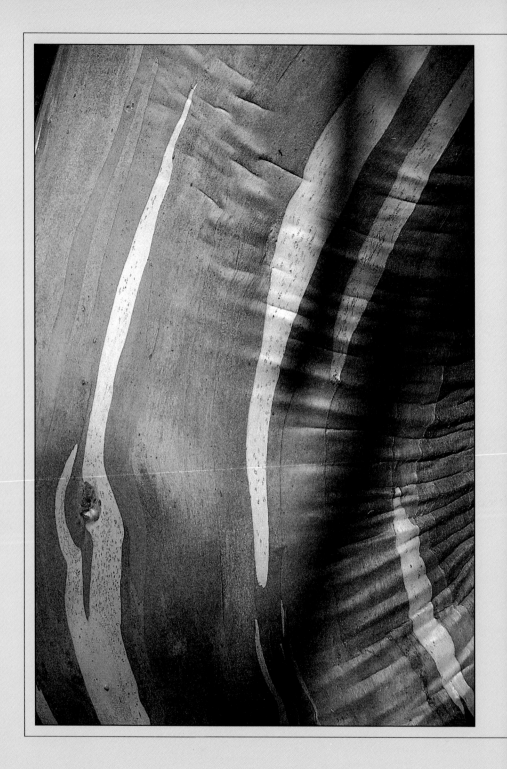

GUM TREE DREAMING

Twisted and gnarled with hardship,
grandeur out of dry ground.
Rugged symbol of our struggle,
familiar with grief and joy.

Rough-smooth arms reaching upwards, lifting
boughs of fragrance, soft explosions of flower;
shedding strips of yourself,
offerings for the earth.

Wounded and scarred from a myriad creatures
who take succour from the life-giving sap
oozing from your beating heart —
bleeding Life-giver.

Laden with healing in your branches,
*   your arms.*
Crushed leaves, sweet scent and touch
of life and strength in my hands,
bruised healer.

Guardian of the rainforest,
sapling torn by wind and rain,
reborn of the bushfire,
revive me again.

SCRIBBLES

Random scribbling patterns etched
in the smoothness of the gum,
Artist-inspired design
in the tree to which I come

in wonder, trace with finger,
pause to linger, touch a kind
of message from a tiny life,
sign of greater work than mine.

Signature of life on life,
pure impressions of live art;
they give this tree a character
that leaves impressions in my heart.

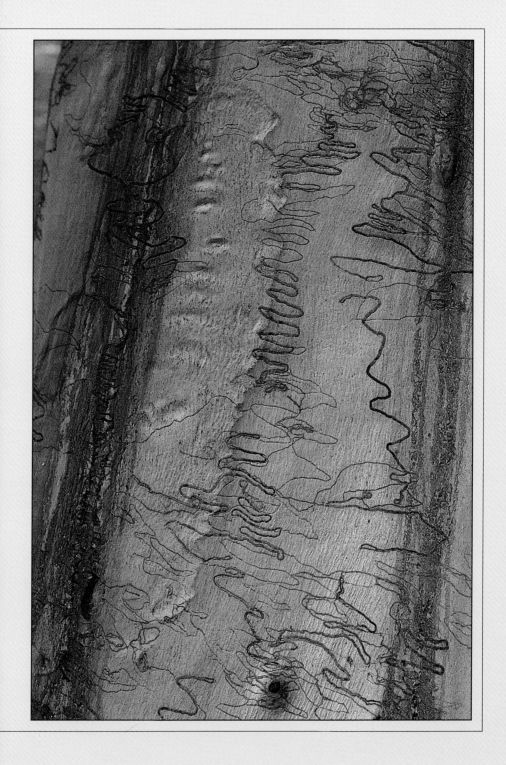

PAPERBARK FRIENDS

Soft sweet secrets
in the quiet stillness standing,
being alone; but I am not alone
in the paperbark forest.
I can hear you whisper to me,
reassuring me in the soothing
*   verdant embrace of expressive silence.*

Touches of soft skin pressed to my cheek,
yielding pieces torn away,
revealing tenderness.
I am vulnerable,
your arms gentle,
and I am a trusting child.

Moving among paperbark trees is like
sharing with closest friends.
Gaining strength through
growing together.
We touch each other in tender places
and it feels like your touch.

Away from here in another place,
when I'm lonely with pain another time,
my footsteps find me finding you once more.
And I am like a child again, barefoot
on soft grass, running into outstretched arms,
in the paperbark forest.

YOUNG GRASS-TREE

When the wind is playing with the sunlight
    among your slender xanthorrhoean
    frond-fingers
    and one happens to be there,
    gazing into your exquisite centre —
an ethereal dance of grace,
    fluid light and shadowrippling greenness,
transcending barriers of thought and expectation
    (Which is substance? Which is light?);
one is immersed in a vision of the spiritual
    in the simple heart of the young,
ascended to another dimension where
    matter is dissolved in a flowing
    emerald realm,
gentle light and shadow the only
    tangible substance.
And Being is a moving, changing, happy
    dance of growth,
reaching upwards and outwards
    and playing with light and air.

HOW DO YOU FEEL?

God, a really sad thing happened today.
A little speckled-brown sparrow flew
*   into a polished window*
and fell at my feet, gasping for breath.
It was a large shiny window of a church,
a very impressive modern church,
*   designed by an artist for really fine*
*   worship.*
I held the tiny bird in my hands, wondering
how I could help to save its life,
but the soft, warm body went limp in my hand.
God, I'm confused. How do you feel?
Such a wonderful little life,
*   formed by your hand.*
And the cars roar past, and the
*   church services continue,*
and the congregation remains standing
*   as the platform party leaves the rostrum,*
and nobody even knows.
But you do. I know you do.
You see every sparrow fall.
And you also said people meant much more
*   to you than sparrows.*
What about the children dying of hunger
*   in Mozambique?*
And the grief-stricken mothers and wives
*   in Chile?*
And the broken Aboriginal families?
God, I'm confused. And sad. Angry, too.
Are you?

RAINFOREST CATHEDRAL

Under towering arches of palms and
　　spiralling vines,
light glowing softly green
through living stained-glass windows,
in the quiet gentleness,
birds calling like tiny bells,
I sit reverent,
humbled by the peace and silence of growth
and the wonder of death and rebirth.

I worship you, Creator of the forest,
gardener of Eden, lover of all hearts.
Cleansed by crystal cold water,
stripped naked by a shaft of sunlight,
human with a dynasty of ugly destruction,
I stand barefoot on the holy ground,
face to face with divinity.

Create in me a clean heart.
Lead me to walk the way he walked —
feet strong but light on the earth,
face upturned for the sunlight,
ears to listen to the many voices,
hands outstretched to touch
　　the wounded gently,
and open heart to love in spite of dirtiness.
Shine your light through my branches, too.

QUESTIONS

God, the questions are so heavy
in my heart today.
What's happening?
What's happening to the world?
What are we doing here?
Where are the plans?
Where are the hearts that really care?
Where are you?
Who can hope any more?
Who are human beings anyway? Who am I?
How long will children keep starving and
the rich get richer?
How long will the koalas, whales
and forests be on the earth?
How much more can earth take?
How much more can you take?
When will the good conquer the evil?
When will the promises come true?
When will tomorrow come?
And how can I voice all the Whys!
How many questions can be lived
in a lifetime?
How many questions can have
the same answer?
How can I know the answer?

RAINWALKING

Waterfalls over me
dissolve troubles that tumble down
into puddles forming at my feet —
rainwalking.

Tiny drops on my eyelashes,
splashes on my cheeks, crying
tears that wash my face with joy —
rainweeping.

Shower for my flesh,
cleansing gift from the sky,
leaving me pure, melting me into the earth —
rainwashing.

Wet hair clinging to my shoulders,
I am singing with
rain-glow on my skin. Celebrating life —
raindancing.

GOLD

We tell stories of how it built Australia,
'civilised' it and saved it from depression.
Shining symbol of wealth and acquisition,
hard currency power to shape and divide
    a nation —
its glitter makes some men sing
and others cry.

But there's another gold that glows
    across this land,
living gold that can't be bought or owned.
Centuries before civilisation, or white man
    and his money,
and still, whenever winter's grey descends
    and settles in,
the wattle shines the brightest gold,
    announcing spring
and making all hearts glad.

Let my value not be measured by
achievement or possession.
But let it be the fragrant living gold
that comes from being touched
by early spring sunshine,
and being made by the hand of God.

EARTH IS SINGING TODAY

Earth is singing today
in the first sunshine after long grey weeks
        of rain.
Thousands of tiny rainbows flash
through the last of the raindrops.

The birds have found new songs
and the grass is whispering the words.
Crickets chirp as if their hearts could burst —
they missed the sunshine, too.

Glistening rocks are alive,
breathing steam as they feel the heat.
Eager lizards run out of hiding
to shine with the surge of the sun through
        their skins.

Green things are visibly growing today,
unashamedly reaching out to light
        and warmth again.
Earth is swelling, stretching its body
under the sun's renewed caress.

The air is charged with the energy of life,
making music for the Sun-maker.
The whole earth is making the music
and I am dancing.

STILL IN THE BUSH

I have learned to pause now and then
from my dizzy business,
to find a smooth warm rock surrounded by bush,
to be quiet and still and wait . . .
Feel the heartbeat of this land,
imagine an Aboriginal hunter stalking silently
*   through the trees,*
the tribe camped over by the creek —
wonder where they are now?
Sometimes stealthy sounds come closer . . .
A crashing through the undergrowth becomes
*   a spine-rippling echidna poking his nose*
*   around.*
A stealthy rustle sends shivers up my neck as
*   a red-bellied black undulates its way to*
*   the creek.*
An elusive lyrebird turns over rocks and soil
*   with big feet, or a clan of tiny blue wrens*
*   flit whistling through the bottlebrush.*
A black-and-yellow goanna advances haughtily,
*   asserting his superiority.*
A shy wallaby family thuds softly
*   through the trees,*
*   or a wary kangaroo tests the air*
*   for strange scents and sounds.*
These other created ones remain in
*   small pockets of bushland,*
and still come trustingly
to those who will be still
and know.

SULPHUR-CRESTED COCKATOO

Today I saw the wildest thing;
it sent my spirit spinning into wild blue space
to soar for an infinite second there.

A screech defying all,
riffle of white against the blue,
wild figure in free flight —
span of feathers cut through
solid air.

Gliding tips poised and spread in flight,
then flicked to spin and tumble.
White bird dance in the air for sheer delight —
catch the sky with span of wing,
ride the wind and touch the sun.

Pure white on blue
with a saucy spray of yellow —
just for fun.

LAUGHTER

The bush waits in hot silence with held
    breath —
even the cicadas are quiet as if listening
    for something;
soundless flight on silent wing, a flash
    of blue feather —
the kookaburras have gathered in the
    tall gum tree.

The head of the tribe starts off with a hoot
and the bush resounds as they all join in
with heads thrown back in the face of the sky —
those crazy laughing-birds are at it again.

Shattering the silence with raucous abandon
in a wild outburst of uproarious laughter.
A celebration of unrestrained mirth
for their Maker and for the earth.

HIGHWAY GRAVEYARD

From somewhere near the stars you can see
      our tracks,
subduing mountain ranges, carving
      through valleys.
Scars across this land stretching
      beyond the horizon,
the grey vein of progress neatly
      marked with white,
metal artery of development,
bloodstream of speed and convenience,
spreading its network, marking a lining
      round this country.

Lining her grey shoulders, sacrifices to progress
lie stricken, silent, limbs stuck
      at strange angles.
Dried blood over once-soft fur, swollen
      by flies and sun,
empty holes in skulls which were
      shy, gentle eyes.
Here the wild met its match at the grey line
and received no burial.
No wonder the tears rain on them — and us.

STILL

In the centre
of this place, of this country,
at the Rock:
boundless dimensions merge into wild focus.
The world stands breathing silently,
and earth is
still.

In the centre
of this time, of this century,
for a moment:
important deadlines whirl and days rock
    dizzily faster,
but some time each will face the quiet
and be
still.

In the centre
of this soul, of this life,
at the heart:
Rocked till I'm empty and stopped
    in stark darkness,
I touch the core and face the stillness
and God is.
Still.

SPIRIT OF THE OUTBACK

It must be a very special part of you
that formed this dusty red, rocky,
    arid-rich place
we call the outback.
Wind-wrecked, hot-cold
endless space by day;
sky-swept dome of vivid colour,
thick blackness, close stars by night.
Stark, lonely,
and yet crowded with a silent,
    screaming presence
that widens horizons
and imparts meaning.
Barren and naked in appearance;
but those who enter this place
find it bursting with life and energy
and power in its heartbeat.
Something is set free within
to soar across a paradoxical landscape
of space and closeness
with the spirit of the One who dreamed
    the outback
and with a sweep of hand
gave it life.

WILDFLOWERS IN THE DESERT

Hot, red, stony land endlessly
breathes out shimmering heat-waves
into deep, endless blue.

Imperceptible wisps of vapour form,
gradually gathering together
until divergent winds whip them into
moisture-laden cumulus,
releasing their precious load
with a burst of rain.

Patiently expectant tiny seeds
on thirsty desert ground,
having survived since last rains,
eagerly burst their skins
and shoot out beneath and above,
lavishly splashing every available space
with prodigal blooms in every imaginable
     shape and colour.

May my arid soul flower in such bright profusion
after seasons of dry anguish and flooding tears.

NATIVE BLOOD

The enduring angophora *tree,*
with its strong smooth skin and wrinkled limbs,
bleeds with native blood when wounded.
Clear crimson pulsing from a heart that
knows grief.

The fragile desert pea,
with shiny scarlet tears dropping out of harsh,
        stony ground,
oozes native blood from parched earth
after rain.
Big wet drops from an aching heart that
knows pain.

The weary, native-born, dark-skinned children
of this land still fight the struggle
that flows and spills the wild blood
        in their veins.
A crimson stream has spilled for us all,
and by the wounds we may be healed.

DOMINION

Human, when you were given dominion
over all the other creatures,
was it intended as power to waste and destroy?
To strip Earth bare of its cover,
choking pure air and water with poison,
razing forests and homes,
    leaving desert wasteland,
raping gentleness and trust,
    spreading disease of fear,
murdering fathers and mothers for sport or
    profit or convenience,
abandoning orphans to die alone?
    Those who are left try to find a place to hide
    and cry silently through eyes of fear. . .

Was not dominion given as sacred duty
*   to advanced intelligence?*
Responsibility for the survival and
*   well-being of all?*
Keeper of the planet's provisions,
protecting homes and families,
respecting mutual relationship with lives
*   different to your own,*
learning from each, enjoying all,
touching with kindness and appreciation,
giving love in return for trust?
*   A few shy miracles still dare to trust our hands.*
*   Can we honour their trust, before it's too late?*

AN EAST-COAST BEACH AT DAWN

There's a pale light on the edge of the sky
*   where it touches the sea.*
The waves have smoothed away yesterday —
*   my footprints are alone on the beach*
as I watch an unseen Artist paint a living skyscape
for the beginning of another day.

White wave-foam takes on a fluorescent glow,
brushes of red and gold merge and flow in a
million hues,
rolling surf tumbles coloured reflections of still sky,
wet sand mirrors reflect subtly-changing
*   colours of moving sky —*
Pure colour and light play with surging water
*   and endless space.*

For an intense moment the colour burns to
*   vivid climax.*
Red streaks blaze deepest red and edge a cloud
*   with brilliant scarlet*
and a ball of gold lifts steadily out of the sea,
dripping liquid fire.

The fireball clears water and stands still for an instant,
and three other beings join me for that perfect moment.
Sleek dolphins leap from water to sky with
*   an eye to the sun, then they're gone.*

The day takes up the colour and light from the horizon,
the beach takes on the footprints of another day,
and I take away the gift of the dawn that I shared
with the dolphins on that east-coast beach.

BEACH BAPTISM

The early morning beach is a still,
liquid reflection of the pale sky.
Only my bare feet touch the calm
smoothness of the wet sand
and leave not a mark behind.

Softly,
a gentle wave reaches up
to wash my feet.

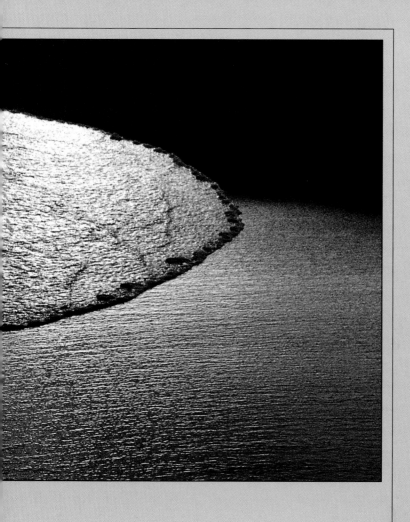

Spirit
surges within me,
responding to the gentle pull of power.

'Not just my feet, but all of me!'
And I plunge into the cool strength
to be buffeted and baptised
by the ocean's waves —
cleansed for a new day.

TODAY'S SKY

Today's sky is delirious with happiness.
The clouds are billowing in all directions,
passing each other in an orbit of exhilaration,
each on its own path,
dancing together but separately.

Their soft white shapes changing,
never staying the same
or following another.

Just carefree drifting on the high winds,
sailing dizzily in the blue,
in a celebration of being
delirious, changing clouds
in today's sky.

ARTIST

*When you are in the storm
of a wild tropical sky,
bursting with full, dark clouds
whipped by high winds into electric thunder,
flinging sheets of water and balls of ice
and flash of fire,*

then torn apart by solid shafts of bright
    hot sunlight
and intense blueness,
radical, changeable, yet utterly unchangeable,
Artist of fire, air and water;
your energy soaks into our dusty spirits
and you feel so close we can touch you.

MY GOD

It's not your words I know you for —
filtered as they are through
a thousand or two years and
a billion or few humanities.
Yet still deep and strong and surging
with such power
that I tremble.

It's not your children —
wrapped up as they are in whirlwind quests for
something meaningful in life, or simply
struggling for some life.
Though sometimes I'm sure they touch me
with your hands
and I weep.

It's not your world —
reduced as it is by the urgency of progress
taking resources for industry, for shelters,
for development, for weapons.
But what remains still so breathtaking,
breathing such life!
I have to sing.

It's something else that fills me with you —
touching all of these,
yet untouchable, intangible, inexpressible.
Union of your soul with mine,
and I know
you're my God.

EVENING BY THE CREEK

When shadows are long and gentle,
and in between are shafts of gold
touching the grass and my hair
and the trees, turning them all
into light —

And the light ripples in gold and deep-green
and silver and indigo on the water;
reflections merge and swirl into pure colours
and the creek is transformed
into liquid magic —

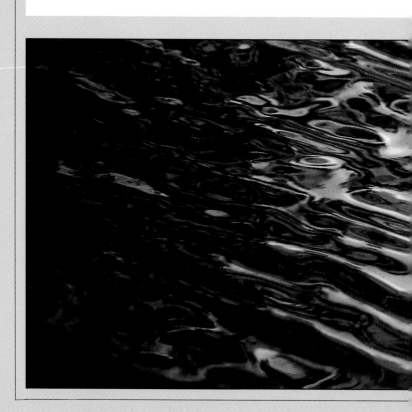

And the birds are playing the air
into softest, clearest notes of wonder,
dancing through the light and shadows,
and then being still, hushed with awe
because the moment is so holy —

And the colour is slowly drawn
up into the western sky over the mountains
where it becomes an orange fire,
and the ancient stars take the light and
*   burn diamonds*
in the deep, dark velvet —

I know you've been here by the creek
*   this evening.*

SUMMER NIGHTFALL

As this night falls,
the stars become live, breathing diamonds,
the crickets begin a chorus of celebration
*   to last all night,*
the soft stillness is a soothing caress
*   untangling the knots of the day,*
and the darkness is a forgiving blanket,

covering the unjust and the
innocent alike.
However the daylight passed,
whatever important business was achieved in it;
its opportunity is over, its sins are enough.
Now it's time to pause, breathe the stillness,
reflect the glow,
and watch another daylight fade beside
the rich deepness of the night.

EVENING SPIRIT

The way
*   the mist*
*   came gently down*
*   this evening,*
*   wrapping the night*
*   around me,*

softening
   the darkness
      to velvet that
         wetly whispered
            against my cheek,
made me
   sense your Spirit
      reaching down
         to touch me
            this evening.

TO DREAMERS

A dream never dies.
It may be buried alive
very deeply,
but has the mystical power
to re-emerge
from the debris
stronger than before.
Some people are locked
in mortal combat
with their dreams,
in an eternal struggle
to keep them buried.
Others let them free,
to lift on powerful wings
into the open sky,
carrying their dreamers
to destinies even yet undreamed.

Location of photographs

Photo taken by Kathy Fook

†*Photo taken by Santo Calarco*

All other photos taken by the author

© Adele Coombs 1992

Published in Australia and New Zealand by
Albatross Books Pty Ltd
PO Box 320, Sutherland
NSW 2232, Australia
in the United States of America by
Albatross Books
PO Box 131, Claremont
CA 91711, USA
and in the United Kingdom by
Lion Publishing
Peter's Way, Sandy Lane West
Littlemore, Oxford OX4 5HG, England

First edition 1992

National Library of Australia
Cataloguing-in-Publication data

Coombs, Adele
Barefoot Dreaming

ISBN 0 86760 168 X (Albatross)
ISBN 0 7459 2196 5 (Lion)

I. Title

A 821.3

Design: Stephanie Cannon
Cover photograph: Adele Coombs
Printed and bound in Singapore by Tien Wah Press